This book belongs to:

Given with Love By:

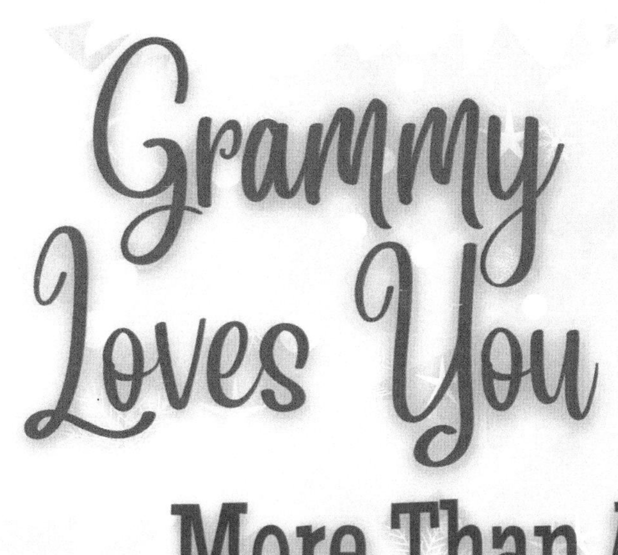
Grammy
Loves You

More Than All
The Snowflakes In The Sky!

The snow was softly falling
from the cold winter sky.

Grammy

Looked up with a twinkle in her eye.

I love you more than
all the snowflakes
that are flying so high!

Grammy
loves you more than
all the
marshmallows in
this hot cocoa mug!

You give the warmest, sweetest, most snuggly hugs!

Grammy
loves you more than
all the bright
morning sun rays.

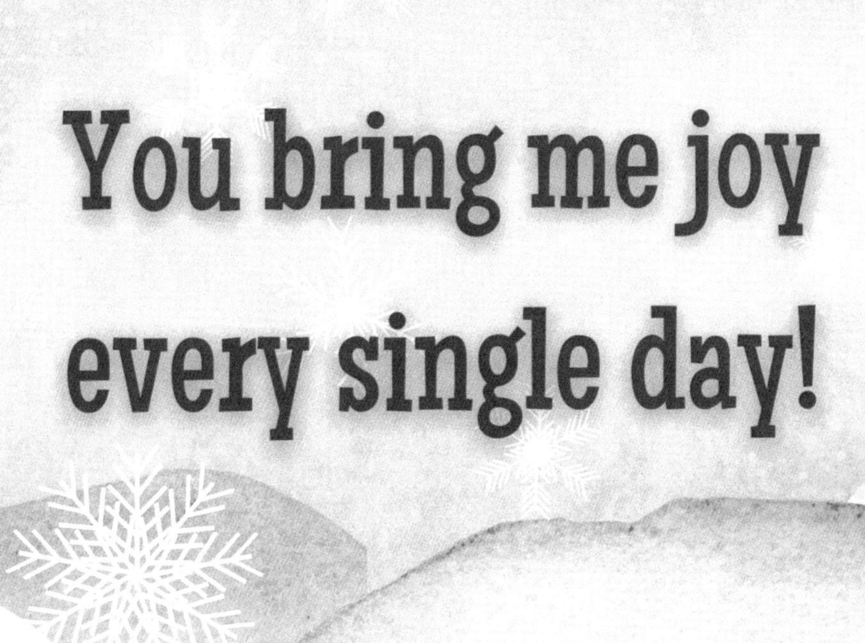
You bring me joy
every single day!

Grammy
loves you more than
all the twinkling
lights!

Your love can
brighten even the
darkest of nights.

Grammy
loves you more than
all the cozy winter
socks!

You make me smile every time we talk.

No matter how many storms cross the cold winter sky.

Please always remember, that
Grammy
Loves You More
than all the snowflakes
that will fly!

Made in the USA
Las Vegas, NV
04 November 2024